THE KINGDOM COMPASS

FELIX IFEZUE

THE KINGDOM COMPASS

Tel +234-8099312271,

+234-80931230007

E-mail: kingdomrealitybooks@gmail.com
felix.ifezue@gmail.com

TABLE OF CONTENT

Dedication

I dedicate this book,

To God Almighty, that is gracious to use me as a pen to write this book.

And

To my beloved wife, Chi Ifezue, that has stood by me faithfully through thick and thin.

And

To all, those are searching for the Divine direction to real life.

Acknowledgements

Thanks to God, for being very gracious and patient with me for 27 years to publish in this book.

Thanks to God for the Ministry of Bishop David Oyedepo that God has used to raise great ministers of the Gospel under whom I served and learned in the body of Christ.

Thanks to God for Full Gospel Business Men's Fellowship International for providing a neutral platform for the expansion of the Kingdom of God.

Introduction

Douglas then in his nineteen, was a young brilliant and award-winning 003 student of a rewound university in America.

With a promising career in front of him in Robotics Medicine, Douglas faces the ultimate test of his life.

He bowed to the central divine command to leave the educational pursuit and move to the bearing of the kingdom compass to a Devine direction.

The news about Douglas decision got to the knowledge of his parents Mr Lorenzo Mandeni and Mrs Laura Mandeni.

That was when a letter from the university was informing of Douglas absence from lectures since he left the school hostel six months ago.

Meanwhile, the feat of this boy stirs darkness within his parents' mental balance.

His struggling mother Laura, who doesn't fully understand what is becoming of Douglas, her first brilliant son, was severely traumatised.

As nightmares consume her, she only hopes that Douglas would come back to his senses and go back and complete his remaining two years in the university.

The daydreams of being the mother of Doctor Douglas, a successful son and an emerging hope for the family were fast becoming distorted.

As days turn over, the dream that she will soon become the mother of the school dropout became her unimaginable.

Meanwhile, her friends are planning to attend the graduation ceremony of their children.

Laura finds herself on a race against time as she searches through her mind to unravel the foundations of this trail.

She unwrapped back each layer of the Douglas life in her mind and could not find any reason why Douglas should be a school dropout.

And just when she thinks she has it all figured out, her predispositions lead her to the most shocking truth of all.

Laura soon realises that she was up against an actual reality about life when her husband got a ring on his phone.

Behold, it was Douglas calling, and he said in an unfamiliar faint cracking voice, "**Dad, please put the phone on speaker mode so that mum can hear me.**

I know you cannot understand what I have to tell you both, but you should try to understand. God has shown me why I am here on the planet and the direction to my destiny.

I am sorry to tell you that I am done with schooling for now and have to move towards my divine direction.

I know you will be sad about that, but that is the way to my destiny.

I have to move fast because I have limited time to meet up with what has been set for me to accomplish. Assuredly you will attend my graduation but not before I am in my divine direction.

Thank you for all your sacrifices", and the phones went silent.

The murky trajectory smelled.

Aching and spasms met.

Life submerged in confusion, unrequited queries, and puzzles with knots of countless uncertainties on the threshold.

And there appears the incredible power on the trap.

Will the light emerge? Douglas, Douglas, his mother, Laura shrieked, to no avail.

Douglas witched off and screened off his parents from his life for four years. It soon proved to be more challenging than Douglas ever could have imagined as impossible conundrum manifested.

His classmates, the university community and parents, were perplexed when the news of his dropout from school is all over the place. Douglas has no tangible justification to show, after three uncertain years.

After seven years, Douglas became the CEO of a multimillion-dollar company in America, providing legitimate services round the globe.

Laura and Lorenzo, now travelling all over the globe in Douglas's private Jet and enjoying the grandiose lifestyle are no more thinking about Douglas graduation.

Life has turned honey and easy, and they receive the monthly credit alert of $4000 each.

The euphoria of watching great coverage of the exploits of Douglas Company in international televisions and media, leave them to a monotonous sentence, "God thank you".

The decisions you make today will start a process of producing a corresponding result.

The Divine direction is not always a smooth ride.

It often presents a mucky and bumpy uncertain route at the beginning, but an unobstructed panorama of hope to the led.

The universe is the original version of a computerised device, programmed and finished by the Almighty Creator.

In it are billions of applications running on their own accord.

What you get out of the universe is the result of the impute you made in it.

There is always a point in life when we find ourselves at a critical junction of life where our decisions must move us in a life direction.

It would not seem to matter much, the direction one chooses at that moment to go, either to euphoria or to pangs of regrets.

But the outcome of those movements is different. One that goes to the west may eventually end up at the beach of Atlantic Ocean, and if he does not stop the motion may end up drowning.

Another may go east until he arrives at a landlocked city of a complex network of roads yet to get to the destination.

The destinations can never be the same. That is a scenario of two different directions, two entirely different goals.

But many times we find ourselves at junctions of many directions to choose from in our personal, family, business and public lives.

In our walk in life, we often turn and face a direction, without clearly knowing the exact outcome of the destination.

Many choices in life are like that. At the time they are made, they don't seem significant.

Those choices you made in the past trigger a series of events which shape your life today. They also affect the lives of your children, grandchildren and generations after you.

There is a way that seems right to a man, but its end is the way of death, Proverbs 14:1 says.

Every day we make choices. And those choices mount up and in the long run, become our life story.

If we could share how we all came to where we are today, at what junctions we took decisions and their outcomes, we would understand where we got it wrong or right.

What story do you want to tell about how your life turned out to be what it is today from what it was before?

I would guess it took a turn when something led you to someone or somewhere that turned around to be who you are today.

The original choice wasn't a big deal, but the outcome was life-changing. Or if you tell how you met your spouse, many of the stories would begin with seemingly insignificant decisions to attend some social event.

That decision led to a relationship which forever affected your life, not to mention your children's lives. Sometimes people make unwise choices which aren't momentous in themselves, but they lead to tragedies.

A young lady decides to have a drink at a party, resulting in her letting down her hang-ups.

She may end up pregnant or with a life-threatening venereal disease.

Since seemingly small decisions can have such momentous consequences, how can we protect ourselves from making wrong choices?

God made man be self-willed but expects him to rely on Him for guidance.

A human being is the most significant problem and enemy of himself.

The man may desire to make the best of decisions the unseen forces pulling on him will not let him. Some of the natural forces working against the man include lust, hunger, envy, greed, corruption, favouritisms and nepotism, and the like.

Because of that, humanity is incapable of making reliable and durable decisions, even in his best mental state.

No one, therefore, should rely on another human for direction to a perfect destination but on the creator whose guidance is superior to any other.

Many relied on the infallibility of scientific precisions and take off only to end up in disasters like air crash, shipwreck, and many unavoidable mishaps.

A friend of mine escaped death by whiskers when he had the urge to urinate and left his turn in ticket cue at the airport.

By the time he came back, the person behind him had bought the last ticket, and the flight fully booked.

He was sad though but took it in good faith and bought another ticket from another airline following two-stop routes to the same destination.

When he arrived on transit at the first stop airport, the news was everywhere that the plane he missed because of the urge to urinate, crashed and all the 240 passengers on board died.

God orders the steps of those on divine directions.

What would your life look like if making those choices of your life direction is determined by the kingdom compass?

Every life purpose has hidden processes which are stages in life to cross on the way to destiny.

Academic qualifications, wisdom, knowledge and understanding are chasing after the wind when it has to do with divine direction.

Divine direction is the exclusive wisdom of God revealed by his spirit to the willing humans.

God does not show people huddles on their way to destiny but directs on how to cross the clusters to the willing humans when you get there.

This book will help you see how to straighten the crooked and count what is lacking in the journey of life.

It buttresses the saying of David in Psalm 127:1-5 that unless the Lord builds the house, the builders labour in vain and unless the Lord watches over the city, the guards stand watch in vain.

In vain, you rise early and stay up late, toiling for food to eat- for he grants sleep to those he guides.

In this inspiring book shows how the choices you make, if aligned with the direction of the kingdom compass, will lead to a life you've never dreamed.

You will see to over 800 divine statements that provide answers to the route to your divine direction.

You need to go through each statement carefully and adopt the ones that address your doubts.

Your confidence will build up in trusting God with your decisions and learn how to read the kingdom compass to know the exact direction to take in your decision making.

Have fun as you read and please write a review to let us know how you feel about this book.

CHAPTER ONE

Steps to divine direction

You will feel as if you had an unexplainable dream when God steps in to give you a divine direction.

God steps in your affairs to give you directions.

You decide to follow divine direction or not at your time and not at Gods time.

Most people are living this life in pains, groping in darkness and moving the wrong direction heading to an uncertain destination.

Life will become divinely entertaining the moment you discover your divine direction and follow it.

Retirement at sixty is not the will of God. God allowed you to live up to sixty to "re-tie" and not to retire.

You start moving to the direction of your purpose when you agree with the divine guidance which may happen in your teens or at an old age.

Some people are not sensitive to understand when God showed the direction to their purpose and went the wrong way.

Age sixty is when to change your ties and tie new styles to start a new job.

God did not create you to die old. He created you to pass away empty.

You have to deliver for the world all he loaded in you. You are going nowhere until you have brought all out.

God is watching and seeing all you are doing. If your way pleases the Lord, He will send a messenger to you.

 If God gives you a message, it is for your lifting. The role of an evangelist is the role of a messenger.

He will remove your problems if you receive the messenger he sends to you and complies with His message.

Your next level is in the hands of God's messenger. Until you meet the messenger and recognise him, you may remain at the same spot.

If God decides to favour you, he will be divinely arranging everything about you. With God, nothing is impossible.

You will operate in anointing if God is your guide. Your oiling will be on your word so that whatever you say comes to pass.

Pride is one of the most significant problems that are keeping most people in poverty. They are always concerned about what people will say.

It is foolishness to be ashamed of you to move in your divine direction and remain in misery than obeying simple instructions to fulfil your destiny.

God will hand over the fruits of obedience when you sincerely step out in obedience to the will of God.

Refuse to beg fellow humans for everything.

If you meet their needs with your gifts, you depend on God to bring them to ask for your services.

The divine direction does not come attractive and comfortable most of the time.

It is better to go Gods way as it is than die in misery.

Refuse to wait forever for opportunities to fly into your hands; it does not happen that way.

Opportunities will meet you on the way if you step out of your comfort zone to search for your divine direction.

Success is a chance, and failure is a choice.

If you believe God, he will show you mercy and let His Spirit lead you to your divine direction.

Your situation cannot be the same again with God shows up on your behalf and works for you.

If God visits his people, mercy prevails over judgment. He will remember His covenant and offer His deliverance.

God offered his redemption gift called Grace, to save us from our enemies, and all that hate us, including ourselves.

God sent you on the Earth to fulfil a specific purpose.

He puts talents in you and expecting you to transform them into skills.

You will remain pregnant until you deliver your goal.

Everybody is pregnant with something that the world has been waiting to see.

The creatures are waiting to see you deliver the world's treasure in your custody.

What is in you is designed with you.

You are unique and custom made for your purpose.

There is no other like you.

Do not be busy pursuing your acquired skills and helping others fulfil destiny at the expense of your talent.

You are a servant king created to rule over your life and to serve humanity with your talents.

The purpose of God for you is not to rule your fellow human beings and use your talents and gifting's to force them to serve you. That is the wickedness on the Earth.

The world will be a paradise if every human concentrates on ruling and bringing himself under control, in obedience to the word of God, serving God and humanity with God-given talents.

The things you see that makes the Earth beautiful are creations of those who used their talents to work for God and humanity.

What else are you waiting to reveal yours to make the world more beautiful?

Many people are preoccupied doing many good things that are not right. The Devil loves such people because they can never discover their Gods given talents.

If you do excellent jobs on the wrong thing, you have not done the right thing.

The right thing God and the world are waiting for you to do is to deploy your talents and gifts to manifest the beauty of God's creation.

Discover your talent while alive.

Do not be counted as those who could not use God-given talents for the world and perished forever in the grave.

At the approach of the expected delivery date (EDD) is, invite the Holy Spirit to handle the preparations and midwife the delivery of your Joy.

Don't force delivery before the time so that you don't have in your hands a bundle of pain. Wait for God's time.

Do not also allow your enemies to be your midwives during your delivery.

 They will frustrate your safe delivery and make you sorrowful if you are lucky to come out alive.

The delivery of your destiny can either be in the "labour room" or in the "favour room".

The choice is yours. Where will you be delivered to your pregnancy?

Favour is the prerogative of God, while labour is of the Devil.

You need the support of God to bring out the beauty of your destiny.

Your gift is the reason why you are born.

To make a living is not the main reason you exist. You are here to make a difference.

Don't be an imitator of others. You are born to be yourself.

You are not making an impact with your life because you must have hidden your gifts or your gift hides from you.

God can hide your gift from you if you are going to waste it if revealed to you.

If you sincerely search and discover your gift, honour will come upon you.

We will depend on salaries working hard to develop other people gifts, which is not why you live.

If you discover talent, you become a consultant and earn more than the salary earners.

Start now to do what you have been planning to do. Procrastination is the graveyard of good intentions.

You will do well if you use your gifts in the time of crisis.

You are deceiving yourself if you are living in abundance from wickedness and ill-gotten wealth, thinking all is well.

Your fate is like the chicken in pen thinking the poultry farmer takes care of it because he loves it.

The Devil is feeding you fat and taking care of you so that those that will eat your flesh will pay him well.

Only a fool will say he does not need God. He does not know himself and where he will end up when his life ends.

You need God to live a fulfilled life because he is the only one that knows your beginning and your end of your soul.

Jesus is the saviour of the world; your salvation can only come from him. If

God favours you, all you do is to wonder how it all happened.

If you deliver in favour room, the angels will announce you. Pray that God will reveal the saviour to you.

It is wise for parents to expose their children to the reality of life, even as a teenager. They will discover their destiny on time if they walk with their elders.

Word of God came to the people in the wilderness and not always to those in the king palace. God can speak to anybody anywhere.

You must change your mindset to have a change of life. The way you live in the function of the information you have.

If your mindset is worked upon by the new information and values, then a new you will appear.

Allowing the fixing of yourself is the only way to see the change you desire.

Self-justification all the time can rob you of fulfilling your destiny.

Yield yourself to wisdom to get salvation.

If not, you may be destroyed by ignorance forever. Love one another and be contended.

The master came to uplift humans with the Spirit of God and fire to qualify them for royalty.

Learn to communicate with God always as the master did.

He was so prayerful that he prayed right from the day he started and at the point of his death.

Be ready to be tempted by the Devil if the spirit leads you into the wilderness. You may need 40 days of fasting to survive the wilderness experience.

For what are you working? What is the God you worship?

And what do you serve and what are your expectations?

It is wise to serve God Almighty the creator of the Heaven and the Earth.

The master started his business after he paid the price.

In the time of uncertainty, pray for a prophet to visit you.

The master wanted to start his ministry in his city Nazareth, but the people there rejected him; he, therefore, went to settle in another town called Capernaum.

You will succeed if you manifest your talent where they receive and believe you. You have to be bold and operate with the power and authority of God.

You don't need everybody around if you want to perform a critical assignment.

Send away those that have no business with your task and allow only those that will help you to succeed.

Evil spirit recognised Jesus. If they see him, they are afraid. If they see you, what will they do and what will you do?

Jesus calling was to preach the kingdom of God to the Lord's chosen.

His ministry entails moving from one place to another. But He did not go outside the territory of His calling.

CHAPTER TWO

The master's direction

After Peter saw a better way of doing fishing business as demonstrated by the master, he left the fishes and all he had and followed him.

Reset your mindset, pocket what you think you know and come the way you are to the master if you believe he will impact your life.

You will receive great results if you obey the words of the master just because it was his words.

If the master steps into your boat for His ministry, your story must change, and you'll see the difference between you and who you are.

The protocol or situation and circumstances preventing you from seeing him, notwithstanding, you can meet the master if you are determined to see him,

Take your offering to God for thanksgiving if the master does anything for you,

Proofs clear every doubt. Unbelief leaves when God demonstrates His power.

Whatever the master says comes to pass, He has the power to forgive sin and heal the sick.

There is nothing wrong with eating and hanging around sinners with the motive of converting them.

They are also children of God. Jesus came because of them.

If the master is with you, you eat and make feasts.

You will labour, starve and become spiritually lean if the master is not with you.

For you to receive the new kingdom life that is in Jesus, you need to renew your life and think like a newborn baby.

Be rest assured that people will plan against you if you do what you feel is right but against their custom.

Jesus prayed to receive approval from God before doing anything. People like hearing Jesus as his word projects power. They got their healing as they listen to him speak.

Among the people close to Jesus were traitors like Judas Iscariot.

In a mixed multitude, you have all manner of people.

The master does not bother about distractions. His concentration is on the alleviation of the spiritual poverty, hunger and sorrow of lost souls.

Beware of the people, love and show them mercy. Treat them well and don't judge them. Don't rely on what they say or can offer you.

See yourself always as one that needs help mercy and forgiveness. Do not consider yourself as one that has arrived. Aspire to be like the Master.

You can do that by total submission to the Almighty God.

The word of God is enough to change any situation. His speech is a command and a decree. The angels carry out His orders. Stand on His name and do as He says because everything obeys His word.

Great faith and compassion move God. Jesus is full of compassion but not driven by our actions and works. The motive behind our actions moves him. Do not let your present situation affect your sense of judgment; be led by the truth.

If you want to be like the master, do what he tells you to do. Then you will be healthy and prosperous. The master teaches and heals the people wherever you go.

Another thing that moves the master is obedience to his word. No matter the situation you find yourself, believe in God.

Let not your faith fail. Do not be afraid and doubt not. Stand on the word of God and do it, he will not let you down.

Do not depend on any man for the solutions to your problems.

God will send the right man to you if you go straight to Him and make your demand clear.

You are in this world like every other person. The choice of life you live and the things you do are your individual choice.

Approach your own life with all seriousness according to the leading of the directions of the master.

Your response to the master's directions is your choice.

Opportunities come in life always, but how you use them is also a matter of choice.

Time and choice avail themselves to all. Give pleasure to the one that called you and not the spectators.

The master came to bring malefactors to God for factory correction.

God looks at the level of your love for Him. Your love level determines your faith level, no him.

Your capacity to love determines the commencement of the rebuilding of your life.

The master warns the people to be mindful of the Devil and his temptation if He had crusades from city to city and village to village.

The cares for riches and pleasures of life take away the power of kingdom life from humanities.

Being patient and having a good and honest heart is the way to keep the word of God in your heart.

Make sure you make proper use of the gifts you have.

The love you see in the kingdom of God is often more than you feel among your biological parents and relations.

The master was a normal man. He got tired and slept. The storm and the wind came when the master sleeps.

If you wake the master up, the storm and wind become calm. Why not wake Him up now.

You can send the Mater to sleep if your fear increases. He wakes up for your sake if your faith increases.

The demons and your enemies don't like the master's presence. If you keep Jesus alive in your life, the demons will run from you.

The Devil does not go into the deep. They want to be on the Earth's surface, causing troubles.

You chase the Devil away if you go into the depth of the spirit and come out with the language they cannot understand.

The Devil is responsible for every one of your wrongdoings. If they depart from you, you will become routine.

Let your immediate household and your congregation know first if God changes your situation.

You retain your miracles if you openly testify what God has done. By so doing you put the Devil to shame and chase him further away.

Signs and wonders attract honour, multitudes and favour.

The master will respond to you if you stretch your faith to touch him.

You cannot trick the master with your physicals and sentiments. You go in peace if your faith touches him.

Do not let the present dead situation around you frighten you. Believe in God, and your status will change.

Why not believe God if he has said the situation would change.

Don't look at the people, their mood and dispositions if your situation is critical. The Devil will use those to deceive you.

Stop looking at the situation but on what God said concerning the case.

Concentrate and believe in God and do what He asked you to do.

Don't give up, no matter what the seriousness of the situation. It is not over until it is over. Even if it looks like it's over, restoration happens.

God sent us to use this book to preach the kingdom compass to redirect the misinformed.

You are to receive a precise bearing to your destination after reading this book. Please keep reading, don't stop until you arrive at your purpose.

Be seriously conscious of who you are. Never offer your body to anybody or anything to destroy.

You can always protect and defend yourself in God using all the affair of faith.

You can only know who the master is if the Holy Spirit reveals him to you.

Many that follow Jesus do not know who he is. Do you know who Jesus is? Do you know him intimately? Are you close to him? Do you know him as one of the prophets?

It has to be a full-time endeavour if you want to follow Jesus. You can do if whatever you do in life is for him. In a sense, you enjoy the full benefits of the kingdom of God here.

If you see Jesus in his glory, the cloud of the Spirit of God will overshadow you, and you will understand the new and the old testaments. That is the only time you hear the voice of God.

Jesus expects us to exercise the power he gave to us. Some wicked spirits are not afraid of the presence of Jesus. They will not leave until you rebuke them with the power he gave us in His name.

You must receive and love one another for God's sake to celebrate in the kingdom of God. In other words, help and encourage other congregations working for the same master to survive.

The spirit at work in a follower is mighty but not to be used to destroy others but to save lives. You may want to follow Jesus, and he may call you by himself, whichever is the case.

The father knows the son more than any other because he knew him from birth. The son should understand the father as well. Do you know your father well?

Who are the babies? They are those that are honest, real and humble. God is looking for babies to receive the saviour. Christ is his son that came to reveal the love of his father to the babies.

You should love you, neighbour, like yourself and care for them unconditionally.

Care for those in need and provide for them if it's in your power to do so. Love your fellow humans just because God loves you to give you what they don't have.

Wherever you see the master, receive him. His presence delivers us from evil and temptation. Be very attentive to hear him what he says.

Don't look at the magnitude of your problems or what you want, hear him first, he is more significant than all your questions.

God lives in Heaven, where the name of the Lord is, that is where his person is, there is his kingdom.

Gods will is where His kingdom is. He provides a daily portion of your needs. He gives the blood to wash to away the sins that constitute the blockade to provision for those needs.

Ask God for whatever you need or want and have.

If you don't ask, you won't have. If you ask God, he will give you Holy Spirit.

If you have the Holy Spirit, you have all you need.

What happens to men is caused by the spirit at work in them.

Dumb man is under the influence of the spirit of dumbness. If the spirit leaves, he speaks.

Life is a game of cause and effect.

Your powers will fail if you are not in unity with yourself.

If divided in spirit, you fail. You will be in total confusion if your body is saying a different thing from your soul and the mind.

Unity of the body, soul and the spirit makes a man of God durable.

Jesus is the son of God, and the Spirit of God works in him.

He that is possessed by the Devil cannot easily escape because the Devil protects him. He will only survive if the higher power of God power comes.

Let your good works be made public.

Let it not be hidden because it may be the light the world is waiting to see. What people see affects their bodies and their lives.

Seeing through the light of the word of God cleans both inside and outside of our being.

If you appear clean outside and dirty inside, you are foolish and do not have the word of God.

CHAPTER THREE

Searching for good personality and attitude

Never turn down invitations, especially if it is meal functions. You learn many things in such gathering and venues.

Tell them the story of what God did in your life when they are in a relaxed mood, gratifying the desires of the flesh.

If you talk, beware of what you say. Men are picking what you say to judge you by them.

What you cannot say in the open, don't speak in the secret because walls have ears.

Always be what you are and who you are.

Mind what you say, when you talk about your master so that you don't speak against the Spirit of God.

God may forgive your actions if you have decided to retune your mindset and become a changed person.

It is a different thing to forgive you if you speak against the Spirit of God.

If you want to talk about the GOOD NEWS, do not bother about what to say, for the spirit will speak through you.

Don't be deceived into thinking that what you have belonged to you. Those things don't belong to you; they belong to God. You will hand them over to Him if you expire and taken away.

What you do with your life is more important than your wealth or what you enjoy.

What you have or want to have are momentary.

Your life continues forever after your human experience.

If you understand the truth about life, you will stop working for things and start working for God.

God will find you useful if he considers you available and ready to be used by him.

Live ready and connected with the Spirit of God. Let the influence of the spirit always be with you.

Always be tuned to Heaven, expecting to hear what God is saying.

The Spirit of God in you receives your benefits or answers to your prayers and hand over to you.

God is always happy with you if you are attentive and prepared to hear him.

If you keep your spirit clouded, you will not hear from God.

Learn to speak even in the cloud of life. God works with what you say.

The master came to take you out of captivity into the kingdom of God. You shall see salvation if you are willing.

To be saved, you shall be willing to forsake all the rebellious and evil lifestyle you learned from the place of captivity and be obedient to take instructions.

Light and darkness cannot mix. They are different from each other and perform various functions.

Light exposes the truth about life, but darkness hides it.

You will live a better kind of life if you understand and guided by these truths.

You may get persecuted for these truths, be rest assured that only the truth can set you free.

Probably the hassles in your business, your marriage, finances or health may have got you distorted.

When you meet the master, you shall be loosed and straightened.

Do not allow tradition or religion to hold you captive in any aspect of life, be loosed and ready for the master's use.

Do you know what the kingdom of God is? It is a great thing that may look so worthless at the beginning, but as time goes on turns into a mighty empire.

You have to be true to gain admission into the kingdom of God.

You cannot be admitted by being religious or being pious.

You must bring the **master** along with you and must be helped by the Spirit of God to gain entry into the kingdom of God.

People and situations may attempt to intimidate you, don't give up.

Be bold and wise not to step out of your firm hold on God because in Him is your protection.

If you are saving lives and doing the work of God, know that not everyone understands who you are and what you are doing.

The master never discriminated anybody, male or female. He was always eating with the Pharisees and the Sadducees.

The master had friends of different people. He teaches them the good news of the kingdom of God.

Be focused because the work you do is not your work but God's. Try always to be humble.

Bring yourself always low so that those that know you will announce you and God will exalt you.

Never do good things for people expecting to be repaid by them. Assist people you do not also know, so that God himself will reward you.

If you want to serve God, you must remove your mind from every other thing and focus on the master's lifestyle. Before you start any venture, plan well.

There is a prize to pay if you want to serve God and want to follow the master. Decide before you do so. You must forsake all you had before and follow him.

Make sure that none of your harvests is lost. Make sure you follow them up. Whenever any of them is missing, go after them and find them.

Kingdom business is a full-time affair in the market place. The capital is Christ, and the business place is the world. The profit is the soul of man gained and kept safe in the kingdom of God.

Celebrate whenever you win a soul, because there is Joy in Heaven.

Don't joke with what God gave you; there shall be no loss of anything.

God has given you your inheritance in blessings. You have them stored in the kingdom of God.

Use the gift of God in your life carefully. The Devil will work to make you waste them like the prodigal son.

Do not spend all that you have. Make sure you save some for the rainy days.

If you lose your divine inheritance, men will hire you for peanuts. You ill beg to live may lose your life in the process. The only way out is to go back to the kingdom of God.

Always rise and feel sorry and decide to return to God if you realise you have not done well. You will be surprised the way you will be received.

Every sinner is a child of God lost to the Devil. A sinner that came back was a son of God that was lost but found, dead but came back to life.

Do not remember the past life of a sinner. Celebrate his coming again to holiness.

God expects us to be wise and to relate with the unbelievers. As we do that in righteousness, we attract resources for the advancement of the kingdom and bring them into the kingdom of God.

You must be faithful in what is in your care. If you do that, people will trust you, want to be like you and entrust more in your hands.

You will be heading to poverty if you lose the confidence of people, and God Himself will not be at peace with you.

Refuse to accept things in safekeeping if you are the type that always falls into trouble if money and valuables are in your care. Learn to say no to be free from temptations

If God sees you have integrity, then He can entrust the riches of the kingdom under your care.

You have the opportunity now to amend your ways to be admitted among the kings.

Royalty will rob on you if you are upright and in the company of kings.

Don't be known as the one that is causing problems and confusion whenever you appear.

If you are such a person, you must suffer in a way that you will not find help from anywhere. Rather be a peacemaker and be peaceful.

Learn always to give thanks to God for every blessing you receive so that more benefits will come your way.

If you have functions to perform, do it as if you are doing it for God and not for man. If you make profits, do not withhold it, account for it. If you do so, personal gains will surely come to you beyond your imagination.

Royalty is among the kings and their kingdoms. It is like the light that shines in the dark, dispersing sparseness. It comes upon you if you are in the company of the kings.

Go after whatsoever you want from life. Push until you get it. You need faith, believing in God while learning from your mistakes.

Live your life as if you have only today on the Earth.

Do the best you can to utilise every second available for you today because you are not sure of tomorrow.

It will be like the days of Noah and a lot if your time is up. You do not know if or how it will happen. It must come, be prepared.

Calm down. Do not look down on any man because you don't know what will happen tomorrow.

Concentrate on your relationship with God. Humble yourself before God and man to be justified.

God can only take you to royalty status if you have the heart of a child and as one that does not know anything.

Your riches and titles will leave you if you die, but you will have eternity if you lived in righteousness with fear of God.

Be wise and submit to God. A wise man does not know everything and continues to learn.

A foolish man is the one that claims he knows everything and cannot humble himself to learn more.

You cannot have life eternal with hard work or religion. You can only have life eternal if you live a righteous life before God.

The master will make you what you should be if you come to him empty just as you are.

If the master sees you so humbled yet full of wisdom, then you will have the privilege to walk hand in hand with the master.

Jesus Christ is the son of God. His body Jesus is the son of man. Jesus was seeing the son of man different from the son of God.

The man in you should have mercy and compassion on another mortal because your body is nothing but a humus soil.

Jesus took time to tell His disciples what will happen to the son of man, but the son of God will recover Him in glory if His time here is up.

The miracle is the product of desires and expectations nursed in the womb of faith.

If you ask anything in righteousness from God, believe you have received it, and you shall have it.

The master knows if you are making efforts to meet him and if you are not.

It will surprise you to see that the master is the one that will come to meet you if you sincerely desire to meet him.

The master came to seek and save the lost that are making an effort to be saved.

The beginning of salvation is the sincere desire to know God.

It is an exciting experience to have a close relationship with the master.

It is at times an arduous task meet the master one on one because many barriers will attempt to discourage and stop you.

You must fight your way through desiring to see him because ordinarily, they will not let you come close to the master.

You must overcome the opposition from the earthly kingdom (the world) to reign in righteousness.

If you have the position, be careful to select whom to work within the assignment.

You must work with people who will help you enlarge your office and not those that will conspire to pull you down.

Remove those that will run you down to let you work well. Hold fast to the opportunity given you, or you will lose it.

Do what the master says if you receive any instruction from Him. He will help you to grow if you do that. Be sure you understand well what the master said. If you don't understand, ask questions.

It is a great privilege to praise God because not everybody can. Even if you don't, the lifeless stones will.

You are privileged to be alive to discover the things that are yours. If you don't, your enemies will deal with wickedly with you and the generations after you.

Utilise the opportunity you have now you are alive.

People will be jealous and will say all manner of things if you succeed in your endeavours. Be wise in the way you talk, check your words.

God is a good God. He loves us and does not want us to perish in ignorance.

God is always patiently waiting for us to change. He has given you enough time, so change and be saved.

Beware of the people around you. Try to live right and mind your words. Try in such a way that they don't hold anything against you. The things of the world are for the world. The elements of the kingdom are of God are for God.

Marriage is of the world; money is also of the world. Both are not issues for eternal life in Heaven.

If you are divorced, do not remarry, and if you do, you commit adultery.

God is interested in your spiritual life. Your human well-being depends on your desires.

God hates hypocrisy and sycophancy. Be honest with yourself, be yourself and humble yourself. Be a servant of all. Make matters plain and clear.

Don't plan to destroy others or bring about their downfall. Help them to come up and to live well.

Have compassion and protect the less privileged.

God weighs what we give to him in proportion to what we have.

Temples built with hands of men shall one day get destroyed. The prayers and praises we offer him start and stop, but the life offered to God lives forever.

There shall be severe troubles on the Earth, but you shall not be terrified if you are righteous before God. It shall turn to you for a testimony.

Unimaginable things may happen in your lifetime but do not be afraid if you live in righteousness.

But you must be patient because, in your patience, you possess your soul.

Your success in this world is not measured in the things you have or have accomplished but on how righteous you are before God.

A day of judgement is coming if God will judge the world. But before then, similar experiences that will try your works will take place in your lifetime or at the moments of your death.

In life, you will see and experience all manner of challenges.

Friends and relations may betray you. In all these, rely on God, they shall all become testimonies.

Foreign armies, physical or spiritual, may forcefully attack and kill innocent souls.

It may be difficult to stop and protect the young ones.

They will all fight back to the best of their knowledge.

If all these things are happening, be prepared for your transition to eternity has come close.

Be on the alert with people around you.

Don't yield your body to them because they are humans.

Satan can enter them if they submit to him and change into wild beasts that never remember you are the one.

Live ready and always be connected to your God because you don't know if your last moment will be. The sure thing is that you must appear before the judgement seat of God.

Try to celebrate the day your name got removed from the book of death to the publication of life. That is the day you obtained your citizenship in the kingdom of God.

Remember also that you got purchased with the precious blood of God.

Your citizenship changed when you got power and the Holy Spirit came and dwelled in you.

If God lives in your spirit, you live in royalty, and your reward is a kingdom. If you have the country, you rule over your life and the Earth.

Don't think you are safe from attack because you are with Jesus.

You need to receive power to protect and defend yourself.

Simon was attacked by Satan while following Jesus. He was with Jesus but did not have Jesus.

Do not think that your interest is protected by association without a defined agreement.

What is in the mind of your associates may be different from yours.

The Devil is at work 24/7, tempting you to offend God.

Be vigilant and be connected to Heaven always so that you do not fall into temptation.

No one wants to suffer pain in the flesh, even Jesus. But if it is the will of God concerning you let it be.

Don't fall into the hands of your enemy under the influence of the kingdom of darkness.

Be watchful and careful because, fear, pressure and circumstances may force you to deny your master.

If you live among evil and mindless people, be watchful and mind your words before you speak. Look up to God for your deliverance.

Jesus was righteous and didn't commit any sin, yet He was accused of violation and killed.

Avoid troubles and trouble makes because you may not know what they have planned against you.

If you have fallen into the hands of your enemy, only God can help you. Just do everything not to fall into the hands of your enemy.

You can be accused of anything and get killed.

The people may use you to settle scores.

Most judgments in this world are passed based on facts by the popular wish of the people and not on the truth. They do that to please people and not God.

Don't be deceived; the wicked can never go unpunished.

Time shall come if in their affluence they shall call for death and it will not come to take them.

Many bear other peoples burden unwillingly just because they carry it by force on them like Simon the Cyrenian. They go about taking the weight of other peoples crosses without knowing why.

Salvation is of the Lord. May the Spirit of the Lord give you the understanding to be sorry for your sins and ask for forgiveness from God and the man you offended?

Speak out loud and say what you want out of life. You don't have what you don't say.

At the moment of death, Jesus spoke out with a loud voice and handed over his Spirit to God by. And so it happened.

The first team of evangelists were women who cared about the body of Christ.

The church leaders may not believe the revelation or direct experience due to your encounter with God.

Keep on working with those revelations, they will understand later.

If the truth is not revealed to you by the spirit, it will be difficult for you to understand.

You must not consent to the counsel and deed of the world for you to be good standing and just before God. The world is evil.

You must be separate from the world and be kingdom focused on becoming a changed person with a new status.

If you are not a kingdom citizen, you will look to see what is happening in the kingdom of God and will not see anything. Even if you see something, you will not understand.

If you don't have a personal encounter with Jesus if you are in the church with others, you waste your time.

You will read the scripture but will not understand if you don't know the purpose of Jesus and Christ.

You cannot understand the scriptures if you don't understand the Good News of the kingdom of God.

The speech is the foundation of everything. God is so much interested in the word you speak because it is the builder of everything around you.

The word can do everything. The sound has life in it. The spoken word of God is the light that chases darkness away.

God sends someone to bring out or activate the word life of humans. If one receives the phrase life, he can now speak, hear and understand.

Everyone came into the world in darkness with closed eyes. The eyes could not see without light in the world.

Words produce tangible things and situations. It carries the glory of God if you see its products.

Jesus did not bring laws to humanity, but Grace. People will want to know who you are when you start talking.

A saviour may be in your midst, but you may know him not.

You may come so close to salvation and remain a sinner.

The first disciple of Jesus was Andrew, but the first convert was Peter. The master administers the spiritual empowerment.

The easiest way to change an offender is "Come and see", and if he comes, he sees proofs of righteousness.

The master will expose you to greater things if you believe and do what he says.

You will know your leader if you see him. Submit to Him to learn more from him.

Do not think you can lobby the master through his mother to see God. Hear him and do what he tells you to do.

At times the word of the master may not make sense to you. His words will bring sense out of your nonsense if you believe what He says to have results.

Do not look at the lousiness of your condition. Concentrate on the word of God in any circumstance of life, even in critical situations. Do what God says, your critical condition will change for good.

Make this moment a time of rededication to God. Change your mindset and lifestyle and put away all ungodly things or activities if you desire the master's direction.

CHAPTER FOUR

The bearing towards the people

Don't deceive yourself into saying you do not know what it means to live a righteous life. You will know if your lifestyle changes for good.

Only Jesus is qualified to tell you about heavenly things because he came from Heaven.

Jesus is an embodiment of salvation. He did not come to condemn anybody but to save everybody.

You shall be saved if only you believe him and do what he says.

What destroys a man is a refusal to come out of bondage. Many are afraid of being exposed because of the horrible secrete things they have in the kingdom of darkness.

The Earth is too large and can accommodate everybody. Keep doing what you came on the planet to do.

Mind your business and stop bothering about what another person is doing in his ministry.

At a time, the ministry of John the Initiator and Jesus were going concurrently.

As John was working in his ministry, Jesus was operating in the full power of Gods fivefold ministry.

The disciples of Jesus were also operating in the ministry of John the Initiator.

Jesus never moved alone but with his disciples.

God does not need your gifts, but if you give him the little and temporal things you have, he will make it significant and permanent for you.

You don't worship God in the physical but in the spirit.

If you worship God in the spiritual, it shows in the material. Physical worship does not show in the spirit.

You have not yet met Jesus; that is why you are still searching for the truth.

Your search will come to an end when you meet Jesus, and he will feed you with his the word garnished with the Spirit of God.

Nobody will tell you if you encounter Jesus. In the kingdom workforce, there are tillers, sowers and reapers.

Most times, you don't let people come closer to God because of your speeches and sermons.

The conversation the convince people to come to God is of the Lord.

God speaks to them through their conscience, and they genuinely believe him.

The master knows how to transform his enemies.

God does the transformation by the truth and life in his work if you believe the expressions of Jesus; you will see signs and wonders.

Signs and wonders make people believe. Religious activities without power in the applied word of God are a mare social gathering. The concept of God is powerful.

Delivering somebody is not by force. It is rational to get the consent of the person because he may prefer to remain and to enjoy life in bondage. Jesus asks, "Would you like to be delivered?" before delivering,

Jesus attends the village feast of his people. When He gets there, he goes to see the less privileged, the sick and ministered to them even those bound by superstitions and traditions.

Many believe you must perform certain rituals and pass through a particular process to gain freedom from the wickedness of the world. Jesus post-paid for salvation and made it so easy that it is by the Grace of God.

Christianity is a way of life they say, but religion is the way of Christianity.

Jesus was sent by His father to express his father's love for humanity.

They that believe and do the will of his father shall live in divine love, and the disobedient shall be damned.

Those that do not love God live to honour the works of men and seek not to honour God.

If you cannot see what God did through the son of man may be challenging to enjoy Gods, love.

The Old Testament was for the coming of Jesus. Every word Jesus spoke is for the salvation of humanity from destruction to life eternal.

Be calm to hear God for He knows what to do in this case, no matter how critical you think the situation is. At times certain things happen to prove your faith in God.

If God asks you to give, give so that the reminder multiplies. If you increased, make sure you don't waste the blessings of God.

Humanity believes in the things they see more than the things they hear. They will tell you "seeing" makes "believing" easy. Man needs signs and wonders to be convinced.

Momentary relief, pleasure and satisfaction prepare you for more torments and pains in the world. Salvation only comes, if you understand and believe the word of God and do them.

Multitudes gather around Jesus every day because he gave them bread and fish. The plan to set him up, but if they see miracles, they marvel and forget their policies.

Jesus browsed through their numerous traps and escaped because he knew if they need fish and if they need miracles.

The word of God is the bread that comes from Heaven given to humanity to eat. Whosoever eats that word and have it stored within shall never hunger again.

Misunderstanding of the person and the mission of Jesus is the most significant problem most people have.

The good news you have never heard is in the understanding of the teaching of Jesus. The good news is about the kingdom of God.

You cannot understand the good news Jesus has for you until you are sure of whom Jesus is.

No man can do the will of God if he does not understand the doctrine of God.

The principles of man are not of God, and most people are following the tradition of men and not of God.

Do not present yourself as a man of God, if it is not entirely your time.

You should know your calling, your place of assignment and your congregation.

You are to work where you are directed by the spirit to be accepted.

Jesus never left the Promised Land throughout His ministry. He was a diplomat and diplomatic when relating with teachers and the lawyers. He tells them what is written in the law-book of the kingdom of God when He taught in the temple.

At all times, do not let position or appearances influence your judgment, be a righteous judge. Jesus knows what is in your heart; you cannot deceive him with your presence and sentimentalities.

Many will not understand you if you speak the mind of God.

The intention of God concerning humanity is the restoration of the kingdom of God.

Do not be afraid of doing the right thing in righteousness. The world will do everything to stop you, keep doing the good works.

No one can lay a hand on you to harm you when your hour has not yet come.

You must be wise to know what to say when you are speaking, what you say may save you or mare you.

Following the words of Jesus is walking in the light. To do that, you must study His ways and His words. Speak boldly. No one will harm you if your time has not come.

If you speak, say what you know. Don't say what you do not know.

Relationship with the master is spiritual. You are dead in sin. If you fail to receive Him,

Sometimes God allows certain things to happen to glorify His name.

In every day of your life; therefore, give God thanks and pray that God will use your situation to glorify His name.

You know you are still in the captivity of the world if you find it challenging to understand and believe the scripture.

You cannot follow Jesus if you are in the detention of the world.

The world order goes any length to discredit the works of God.

God intervenes in the affairs of people only if they ask for it.

If anybody who worships God prays, God hears and answers, but He does not honour the prayers of a sinner.

Mindblindness is worse that eye blindness.

There are enlightened foolish people with open eyes but cannot see. Until a man's eyes are open to the truth of the scriptures, he remains in darkness.

You can answer for yourself from your experience with God if you are of age. Be ready to talk about it anywhere.

Jesus will reveal Himself to you if you believe in his word and works. But if you don't, you remain in captivity.

Many are struggling to enter Heaven to see God if they have not done what they are on the Earth to do.

They may not see Him in eternity if they do not locate the truth about their lives before their time is up.

If you discover the master on your side, then you are protected from the captivity of the world.

You have the power to lay down your life to God and allow Him to make you.

You also can take your life from God and be what the world will enable you to be.

Jesus was focused on His ministry and was able to accommodate all type of character in his ministry.

He was never distracted by Thomas and Judas because he is the resurrection and the life. He specialises in giving life to any dead situation.

Human beings like to believe facts and not the truth.

They don't know that not all events are the truth and that all truth is facts. The easiest way to see the truth is to believe the word of God.

Jesus had a special love for Mary because she shepherds to Him. The extension of that love got Lazarus brought back to life.

There is hope now for you as the master is handing you case.

The master knows how to glorify the name of God solving the problems of men.

You may think the death case is over, but to Jesus, it is not closed but sleeping.

Jesus will wake up all your dead cases to glorify God if you believe.

If Lazarus the brother Mary and Matter died, the people thought he was gone forever. With Jesus, no case is closed.

No matter how far your case has demented and maybe you have lost hope of jacking back to life. All you need to do is to believe that with God, all things are possible.

Many like to be very emotional in the face of challenges.

Emotions and regrets cannot solve any problem.

The way out to solving problems is to face the problem with what God says about it.

Man often needs physical proofs to believe. But "by faith, all things are possible" is the real believing.

The way to win battles is to come forth with testimonies how you have won the campaign by the word of God before the fight starts. These attitudes send your worst enemy far away and lose you from the bondage of the world order.

Many are jealous if they see your success coming and will do anything to stop it, be careful.

Caiaphas said a word that took the life of Jesus but brought about the salvation of the world.

There is high power in spoken words. The speech you made can save a nation and can set them ablaze.

Wherever you are, watch out the characters around you.

Caiaphas prophesied the death of the master, Martha anointed his body and Judas demonstrated his love for money.

When Jesus knew they were planning to kill Him before his time, He started avoiding the Jews.

Don't yield yourself unto the hands of your enemies. They may destroy you if you don't adopt a Devine safety strategy.

In a gathering of people, there are many characters and motives.

Everyone has his views and opinions, be careful and watchful.

People will naturally be jealous of you if you are doing well.

As long as you can work in righteousness, keep doing well and focus on fairness.

They will do everything to stop you but be focused and continue serving God.

As you keep working for God and not yourself, people will be coming to seek God through you.

It is wise to change to new and better life experience than dying in wicked living and goes to suffer forever in hellfire.

Many believe in the word of God, but because of what people say refuse to embrace the truth.

Naturally, praise gladdens the soul of a human being.

Jesus brought the world to light by the establishment of the kingdom of God.

You believe God If you believe His words.

Without the word of God, you die in darkness.

God will judge every man on the last day base on your obedience of His commandments.

God is a relentless lover of human beings. He sent Jesus to show how dearly He loved the world.

When Jesus left, he expects us to love one another the same way God loves us. So like everyone unconditionally to show them the love of God.

The Devil is the master planner of all evil.

The Devil has no legal rights to operate on the Earth because he has no physical body and works assiduously to hire the body and mind of the human being to perform.

The Devil uses your brain some time to work against you and does evil on the Earth.

The kingdom of God is for master servants. It is for those kings that are always ready to meet the physical and spiritual needs of the people.

You admit Jesus to prepare you for leadership if you allow Him to wash off wickedness from every part of you.

The master will clean you up to make you ready to receive the Holy Spirit that will lead you into all righteousness.

Wash others clean from iniquity also with the word of God as Jesus washed you by his name.

The master brings closer to himself those he loves than the others. Those are spiritually connected to him more than the others.

Those that get spiritually connected to you are the people you should bring closer to you more than the others.

The master activated His glorification by giving a sop to Judas his betrayer.

You must identify your facilitators and enable them to move you to the next level.

Don't ask too many questions if you follow the master because you cannot understand everything He does.

All you need is to believe God is that the Holy Spirit will give you understanding.

Your righteousness cannot be complete until you learn to love your fellow human being as Jesus did.

If true love is not in you, then you are just religious and not serving God.

You must believe in God to live a fulfilled life.

You cannot understand God except you know who Jesus is, and cannot relate with God except through Jesus.

Jesus has gone back to his home in Heaven and is no more physically in the world.

You cannot point at any man on Earth and say that he is Jesus but his word lives. You can always relate to Him by referring to his words.

You can only survive in righteousness if you always connect to the master via his word. It is only then you enjoy your rights and privileges in the kingdom of God.

Jesus never asked anybody to pray to or through him.

He asked his followers to pray in his name to our father and his father, the God almighty.

You can never be higher than the master.

The master can do what we do, but we cannot do what he did. That made him the greatest of all times.

We need to submit and always work according to these words of the master.

The world will not love you because you follow the teachings of the master.

They will come to seek help if they see the impact of his words in your life.

Do not let the wickedness of the world stop you from speaking the truth.

The truth the people hear will judge them. The Holy Spirit will confirm the master, and you give evidence of him.

You commit iniquity if you don't live according to the word of God.

Our righteousness is Christ in us. You cannot be righteous if you don't know what God says.

Holy Spirit is for us what Jesus was to his disciples while on Earth. He stands now between Jesus and us.

God has already adjudged Satan.

The Holy Spirit will bring you to the judgment declared any time you meet Jesus with the Joy of your victory.

Jesus was praying for humanity before he showed us the way to the father. But now we have known the way; we can always reach the father in His name.

Time may come when everybody abandoned you and go their own way. Thank God if such happens.

People to abandon you may be in God's plan to send them away to have a quiet time with you. That may be the beginning of your lifting.

Jesus came to save everybody from the wickedness of the world. He has provided salvation to those who want to be protected and gave them eternal life.

The wicked powers of this world deceive those that refused divine protection.

Jesus prayed for the salvation and the kingdom citizenship of for all humanity all over the world.

The instrument of salvation is the good news of the kingdom of God.

The master surrendered himself to the will of God if he finished his work on the Earth.

Leave the rest to God if you have done your part.

The physical weapons cannot win spiritual warfare.

Every battle has appropriate ammunition required for the combat.

Fight the spiritual battle with the complete armour of faith.

Locate the truth about your life before your time is up.

If you discover Jesus, then you are protected from the captivity of the world.

What accusation do you have against Jesus? If you don't have any then why not believe Him and is saved?

Your closest friend maybe your betrayer tomorrow. Be watchful.

Jesus spoke the truth in the open. Everybody heard him and said his word is right.

Whatever you say concerning Jesus, is the much you know about him.

Go and learn of Him. If you give your life to Jesus, he will defend you at all times.

Most religious people try to fight for God. How can you fight for the creator of the universe?

Fight spiritual warfare for yourself, and God almighty will manifest your victory.

Everything will fail you at your last moments on Earth. Be wise now you still have breath and strength to be introduced to Jesus.

You will realise if that time comes that the only one you will need is Jesus.

Jesus is the king of the kingdom of God.

The kingdom of God is not like the kingdom of the world. It is the presence of Heaven on the Earth.

When Jesus finished his evangelical and apostolic work, he went into a garden.

They betrayed the master and took him from there to false judgment in the location called the skull.

Jesus was firm at the point of his judgment by the world.

The world is in darkness and confusion because it preferred the robbers and the thieves to Jesus.

Pilate knew that Jesus was the king of the Jews. He released Jesus to die to retain his Roman appointment.

The coat Jesus was wearing was extraordinary; that is why soldiers desired to take it.

While all the men went into hiding, the women were very bold and came close to the grave of Jesus and identified with him.

You cannot say you have finished your work on the Earth if you have in you the treasures what belongs to humanity.

Jesus never said he finished his assignment until he gave out all he had in his life.

Everybody went into hiding at the time when the body of Christ was undergoing persecution.

What are you doing to save the body of Christ from abuse?

Joseph Arimathea rose and did something to save the body of Christ from being abandoned on the cross.

Joseph requested the body of Christ for safekeeping.

Use your connections to work for the body of Christ when you are in a privileged position.

Also, Nicodemus appeared to add a sweet smell to the body as his contribution to the body of Christ.

After they kept the body properly, then the women came to take care of its proper preservation.

What are you doing for the body of Christ?

In the body of Christ, women take time to dig out information. Still, the men will always take time to verify the information before they act on them.

Men always gather if the women reveal information and do everything to understand what had happened.

In the heat of any situation, men will act and leave, but the women will insist on finding the beginning and the end.

Women are very daring when it comes to pursuing a case; they must continue seeking until they get to the end of the matter.

The women are more committed to keeping watch over the body of Christ.

The make sure that the body of Christ is safe and not taken by the wrong hands.

The women insisted until Jesus appeared and gave them the first message after His resurrection.

Many are bootlickers if it comes to working for the master.

The sycophants do everything to show they are working hard when the master is around.

When it seems the master was no longer around, the flatterers went back to their wicked ways.

The master will always locate the bootlicker in his wickedness because he comes, again and again, looking for the master when things around him become tougher.

A backslider will always be ashamed in his backslidden state to meet the master because of a guilty conscience.

Many pretend to love the master when they are with Him. Immediately they leave his presence; they go back to the wild.

The teaching of Jesus Christ is the restoration of the kingdom of God. This kingdom is the gift of God to humanity.

That promise of God is worth waiting for patiently because it cannot come to you if the Holy Spirit does not deliver it to you.

Do what you can now that you are alive because time is fast leaving you behind.

When you become old, others will decide what you should do.

Do not bother about what others are doing and how fast they are going on the planet. Mind your business to fulfil your purpose; everybody shall end at the same place for judgement.

CHAPTER FIVE

Bearing towards the leadership

Only an ignorant person can see the universe and the frailty of his being and say there is no God.

The master came to show humanity how God is and the intensity of His love towards him.

The good master established a kingdom whose foundation and governance is according to the direction of God.

The master's job is to teach and to do the necessary things for the followers whom he instructs by the power bestowed on him.

The master does not stay with His followers forever.

The master leaves to higher responsibilities after training his followers to continue from where he stopped.

Restoration of the kingdom comes with the supreme power provoking the power for observation.

The folks living together in unity in the upper room, acted together before they got the power.

Out of every twelve, there is a Judas, but the reward of iniquity will kill him.

The crowd in most gathering is critical, but the power of unity determines their strength and not the attendance.

If you want to relate with God, intimately, stay in one place and one accord with yourself.

Unity of purpose is what love is all about, and it attracts Gods attention to everything you do.

Crave for and expect the infilling of the spirit, which is the presence of God.

If you notice the presence of the Spirit of God, speak out and remain still to hear in your language what He is saying to you.

If the Supreme power controls your life, many will not understand you. They will think you are drunk.

Ordinary men are confused if the Supreme authority of God acts.

If you see blood, fire, vapour and smoke in the kingdom, there is danger.

In strange times like that, whosoever calls upon the name of Jesus and act swiftly shall be saved.

Jesus Christ is the only prophet that did not leave his body in the grave.

The master took his body and went back to God.

The religious and belief founders went into the tomb and never came out.

It was only Master Jesus that went into the tomb and spent three days and came out alive.

The Supreme Power of God is there for everyone who repents and accepts the work of salvation of Jesus.

There will be oneness, fellowship and gladness when you meet the real needs of people in a relationship. They will praise God more and will have a favour and increase in number to support you.

Look at your helpers closely to see what makes them your helpers.

The worst thing the Devil hates to remember is that Jesus came back from dead and escaped.

What brings salvation to man is the name of Jesus and reminding the Devil of the power that brought Jesus out of the grave.

God can use anybody to preach the Good News; it is not the prerogative of the pastors.

The kingdom of darkness may threaten you, but in the name of Jesus, you will be set free. Always praise God for that privilege he gave to humanity.

The kingdom of God is a commonwealth. No one lacks basic needs because they own everything in common.

It is a dangerous thing to lay to the Holy Spirit, and many "pastors" are doing just that putting the church in dishonour.

Christianity is supposed to be an open demonstration of power and glory to God through the preaching of the kingdom of God.

The shepherds in the early church were honest and were treating everyone equally. There was no racism, tribalism or nepotism.

When the leaders are open-minded, the Holy Spirit works with them. The spirit will perform great signs and wonders through them. That is what makes congregations increase in population and wealth.

Seeing great signs and wonders, the people will so much believe in their shepherd that they positioned the sick by the roadside, considering getting help if his shadow cast on them.

Everybody that came to a love demonstrating church received emotional and physical healing.

The shepherds were apolitical and not afraid of the government. The angels are always fighting for them.

The shepherds were preaching nothing else, but Jesus resurrected and glorified. The Holy Ghost was with them, and many believed.

The Gospel of the kingdom shows in the life of the citizens and not necessarily by preached everywhere.

They must complain when the ministry grows. The minsters should not neglect such complains but address them.

If such complaints arise, set up a committee of mixed groups to take care of the welfare of everybody, the work belongs to God and not to any man or group.

If the congregation is orderly, everyone gets involved and

marginalise no one. More people will join, and the ministry will grow.

In trying to convince someone to change from evil to good, please be straight and specific. Tell the real-life story with examples of what happened for the potential convert to see and believe in God.

Conversion is changing somebody from evil to a proper way of living and not persuading someone to change religion or group to join your group.

Make sure you don't bore people with long scripture stories and don't use abusive words.

Don't get your audience angry and offended. Just let the gathering know that God loves them and express that love by demonstrating the life of Jesus.

Let them understand the meaning of the kingdom of God and help them to appreciate the love on the cross.

Saul was indeed the main person that killed Stephen. The same message of salvation preached by Stephen was the same Philip taught. Their methods of preaching were different.

But after hearing Stephen, they were outraged and killed him. But when they heard Philip, joy-filled their heart and great miracles happened.

Don't be afraid of anybody, and don't lose focus, keep doing what you do While labouring to change people's lives. Don't try to impress anyone. God knows what to do for you.

Beware of brethren like Simon in the congregation their motive of believing is different.

Many believers have not changed. They believe but have not changed their way of life like Simon.

To be Christ-like must first be desired and take positive steps to become.

Confession shall be made in public and follow it up with repentance from the evil way of living and start a new life.

God is particular and explicit if he calls somebody to do specific things. If one desires to know God, God reveals Himself.

The eyes of a truly converted person are blind to the world and open to the things of the spirit.

God can choose anybody to do a work for Him Paul is a typical example.

They that are the faithful followers of the Lord are in variance with the world. The world will not understand Him.

Signs and wonder is the easiest way to make people believe. It remains a powerful gift to convert people. Seeing makes understanding easy.

God is the God of every human being.

God loves all that fears Him, and live uprightly irrespective of religious creed or belief.

God will relate with you if you love your fellow human being with compassion and righteousness.

Be terrified of God, and living upright is not enough.

Feeling loved by God is not sufficient. In addition to this is your salvation from the world, which is more important to God than all those.

Do not treat anyone living a good and a Holy life as common or unclean. You should tell him what to do to gain salvation.

Christ is still moving the streets of the Earth, saving those that accept Him.

God does not prefer anybody more than the other.

As long as you fear God and live uprightly, He will accept and rescue you. You must be a kingdom citizen to be protected.

If God sends you to change the criminals, go and do what he asked you to do for them.

If you go to the criminals by yourself, be careful because they may transform you to become one of them.

God has also given diverse gifts to every man on planet earth. He gave you those gifts for restocking the planet earth.

The gift of God to humanity is Heaven on the Earth.

Salvation is to anyone that accepts nationality—citizenship for that Heaven on the Earth given free of charge.

CHAPTER SIX

Locating the shepherds and the flock

The early ecclesia cried to God in prayers any time they were persecuted and was delivered.

If the children of God keep quiet and do nothing now, the enemy will attack then again after the previous one. But with prayers to God and swift reactions, the saints can stop the enemy's molestations.

God will hold the captor of the saints' captive, and everything about them will change if God steps into their affairs.

Everything that God created gives Him splendour. God will let the saints know that He is their God, the creator of the universe.

If you think we are what we are by ourselves and not by His mercy, the attacker will attack again.

Everyone has a call of God in His life.

The land of the Jews is a land of seven nations God drove away and shared to twelve tribes of Judah.

God may be preparing you with your present life experiences for the future works want you to do.

People will be desirous to hear from you if you find yourself in a place of your calling. Others who came to such an area may be there before you, but if you appear, they will fade away.

It may be very dangerous to expect God to do your will. You can do your will, but the will of God is supreme.

It is safe and right to do the will of God. The intention of God and the will of man are not the same.

Paul's ministry was not for the synagogue but the people out there. He was an evangelist called for the freethinkers.

The hallmark of the preaching the good news is the re-establishment of the kingdom of God. Paul's calling was to preach the Good News to the non-Jews.

You have no business with persecution if you are in the place of your calling.

The people start revolutions against Paul and Barnabas each time they preached the Gospel in the synagogue. Paul is not for the Jews but the gentiles.

Paul enjoyed exceeding support whenever he preached the Gospel among the gentiles. There is a glory to God each time Paul was in the place of his calling.

Paul never allowed his converts to backslide. He follows them up consistently and visits them from time to time.

The most excellent instrument for evangelism is stories of tangible things

God has done and is doing in the lives of people.

The stereotyped attitude of worship (religion) is a virus and satanic instrument to destroy the kingdom citizenship of the people.

Their customary laws and traditions are yokes on the lives of potential kingdom citizens.

Follow up is the cornerstone of soul winning. It is the instrument used to measure how your converts are doing.

The Holy Spirit can forbid you to preach the Gospel to some people, and you may suffer persecutions if you insist.

You might lose your place and not be accepted back in an established work if you departed from activity when it was at the forming stage.

In Christianity, you don't do a work you are not released by the Spirit of God to do.

God will always tell you if he wants you to do work in a place.

God opens the heart of whosoever that fears and worships him to know him.

The heart receives the Good News, but the spirit of divination is a possessing spirit from the Devil that takes it away.

Diviners can see things and say things but have no solution to problems. It is dangerous to fall into the hands of diviners.

The Lord will always defend you whenever you are on the right course.

You will become a sign and wonder when God steps into your affairs, and every mess in your life shall become miracles.

The shepherd can transform lives and take them along in his missionary. He takes care of the flock, and they increase in number.

God is faithful without injustice. He is right, perfect and upright and all His ways are righteous and just.

The freethinkers will entice people to stand against the Gospel and do anything to discredit the good news.

The Berean Christians search the scriptures daily to confirm the teachings of the preacher. You have to do like them to be worth the sitting under the preacher.

Let the scriptures be the base for each of your discussions. Let it form the cores for your actions.

The disciples operated in wisdom whenever they discover their teachers threatened while they work to protect them.

The Jews were the main opposition to the Good News of the kingdom of God.

They were always organising people against the Gospel. But God will not be comfortable with those at peace, seeing people living in bondage.

You have nothing to give to God because everything belongs to him. God wants you to seek Him, to find Him and feel him with what you have.

Do you know the God you are worshipping? Many do not know nor understand the God they worship.

Are you sure you are not religiously worshipping the unknown God?

Some will believe and be saved while others will not and remain in the world of deception if you tell the truth about the world, but the precision remains the truth.

Even the most challenging person to convert will believe you if you are in the place of your call.

You will always hear from God, and no one can hurt you if God assures you of his presence,

You must understand the link the Old Testament has with Jesus as the Christ. That will help you to understand the depth of God's love for you.

John the Initiator is the link between the old and New Testament. Good knowledge of both testaments will enable you to bring a man from his old nature into the new.

A half-baked leader will raise half-baked staff.

An organisation cannot grow more than the spiritual level of the administrator.

It is dangerous to sit under a half-baked pastor.

Initiation by water is the initiation to introduce you to a new of thinking or the Baptism of John.

The initiation of the Holy Spirit is the Baptism of Christ. In the presence of the Holy Spirit, you see signs and wonders.

You will magnify the name of the Lord if you see signs and wonders.

You will believe the scriptures when you experience the manifestation of Gods power.

Every shepherd on duty should be vigilant and intelligently watching the move of God in His domain.

Some do not have the Holy Spirit and perform magic wonders. From such people flee. It is only the Holy Spirit that shows signs and wonders.

You need reasonable intelligence gatherings to know what is happening around the church if you are a pastor.

The enormous opposition to the Gospel in the tradition of men, which is the way they do things. It is difficult to change the culture and tradition of men.

You require a new kingdom culture and the Holy Spirit to change the tradition men to heavenly culture.

The reason many find it difficult to change their mindsets is the earthly benefit they think they enjoy. They don't think of the foolishness that befalls them on their last days.

People are afraid of losing their belongings if they change, but they end up losing them at the end of their life and arrive empty in Hell.

At times there may be dissatisfaction in the congregation. Invite the Holy Spirit to intervene in times like that, give thanks to God and go ahead with your works.

Commotion may ensue in the congregation. Just be calm and look unto God to bring comfort and continue. Never be demoralised by anything in the work of God.

As a shepherd, you must be prepared to face diverse challenges. Some of the problems may be so frightening that you may be contemplating abandoning the work.

But be careful before you entirely because you may end up drowning in the waters if you jump out of the boat.

As a minister, you should understand that the Devil is working hard to spoil your testimonies.

You must possess the humility of the mind. Intensify your work and withhold nothing from the brethren.

Be careful to understand that you will give an account of the flocks over which the Holy Spirit had made you an overseer.

The congregation of God is purchase with the precious blood of Jesus.

You should also know there are people in every congregation who are looking for an opportunity to discourage other members.

The distractors would want to exploit the new members and send them back to wickedness. The owner of the work will always help you.

Have multiple streams of income to have enough to provide for your flock

Every shepherd must have a clear vision of how to keep the flock alive.

It is essential to raise an assistant recognised by the congregation that will always stand for you any time you are not with the group.

The flock is empowered as they increase in number. Many may try to behave like the Pastor.

From time to time, many in the congregation may be missing. The missing ones are sought and found as the voice of the shepherd becomes more evident.

Innovation in ministry is essential to upgrade the keeping of the flock to have a better result.

Always inspect the congregation periodically to know the state of the people.

The Church of God is the people and not the building. 90% of the church resources should go to the people.

A minister should hear from the Holy Spirit to know what to do at all time.

There are things you may want to do which the spirit may withhold you from doing.

God speaks severally using different ways to avert problems in the congregation. He speaks through the prophets and the scriptures.

A shepherd can be beaten by a mob and arrested by soldiers if he disobeys and do what God asked him not to do.

As a shepherd of Gods flock, avoid trouble like confrontation with the ruling powers in your location.

Confront them spiritually if need be and with the demonstration of the power of God. Let them see your light and glorify your God.

Confrontation with ruling powers may cost the shepherd a lot of embarrassment and harassments. Only God can deliver him from such.

No principalities, power or authority can withstand if all the shepherds of Gods flock come together as one in a holy assembly backed up with the action as directed by the Holy Spirit.

Demonstration of power, signs and wonders backed up with the word of faith sustains, increase and empowers every progressive congregation.

MY NOTES

<u>MY NOTES</u>

<u>MY NOTES</u>

<u>MY NOTES</u>

<u>MY NOTES</u>

<u>MY NOTES</u>

<u>MY NOTES</u>

<u>MY NOTES</u>

MY NOTES

<u>MY NOTES</u>

MY NOTES